Business Programming Techniques

New Business Intelligence Theories and Paradigms

Durga Madiraju

Business Programming Techniques
Copyright © 2025 by Durga Madiraju

ISBN: 979-8894791197 (sc)
ISBN: 979-8894791203 (e)

The Reading Glass Books
BOOKS

The Reading Glass Books
1-888-420-3050
www.readingglassbooks.com
production@readingglassbooks.com

Contents

Business Rules – Part 1

CHAPTER 1

Business Rules – An Overview

The business rules in different areas of software application architecture and implementation are presented and discussed for a perspective of business rule failures. The author undertakes a comprehensive search of all major search engines as well as multiple databases to examine in detail business rule failures, using literature review to support the cause of business rule failures. The author examines business rule failures and improvement measures for cases of failures using software construct synonyms such as business requirements, design, l prototype, test, implementation, and post-implementation. These failures are studied through new theories such as data segmentation theory to segment data marked as failure for improvement scenarios, data isolation theory, to isolate particular instances of business failures, data regeneration theory to examine failures through regenerated data, and data overlap for overlap of business requirements using business theories.

Business Rule Definitions

Business rules are directives that define business activities and are a requirement for the business flow of an organization for the efficiency, consistency, and predictability of business (Raia, 2019). Business rules provide guidelines on how an organization must conduct its business. Business rules outline relationships between objects and guide decision-making (IBM Cloud Education, 2021). Some examples of business rules include control documents (a document such as a business requirement for a subscription renewal of a customer membership process that must go through a business requirements review for implementation), processes (a series or a sequence of steps such as a defect improvement process that needs to be mapped to a future value stream process for prevention of defects (describing a value improvement process to reduce defects or wastage in the current process), definitions (a statement or a construct such as a rule defined for the different statuses of customer requirement flow, to define product flow of different channels, and summarize what the definition accomplished), and limitations (restrictions of a rule such as a rule that a product must be sold only at a certain price as otherwise it would cause a failure of a process in a value stream map). Some Examples of business rule failures for product orders include wrong refund of orders made to customers, wrong cancellation of orders by customers, business rule manuals for use by a CSR not current, a rule that was correct but was interpreted and applied incorrectly, a rule that was defined wrongly, but was applied, and resulted in a failure because of a system error(s). The study also cites examples of business rule failures of Education Facts business rules. The business rule failures of Education Facts system includes 5-year edits to data, dropouts, match, lunch, membership rules, ccd school performance, submission rules, wrong grades submitted, incomplete graduate completions report, format failures, and other types of business rule failures. The business growth of a business must use a framework of business rule methodologies and is dependent on the successful creation and implementation of business rules.

Origin of Business Rules

The business rule approach can be traced back to (Business Rules Group, 1989). This approach can be supported with business rule examples such as, a business rule to identify duplicate customer name(s) or a business rule to identify different statuses of a customer order such as an order submitted, order held, order completed, order rejected, and various others. The business rule approach emerged from a driving force to support business practices. The approach was the vision of dedicated professionals with several years of experience using trials and challenges of business software. In 1990, a consensus emerged from the originators of business rules for the business rule approach for business rule terms, facts, and rules. The business rule mantra was a report of the GUIDE of business rules project and was published in the 1995 paper. The principles of the business rules approach was codified in the business rules manifesto, a 2003 work product of business rules available in 12 languages (Business Rules Journal, 2020). The semantics of business vocabulary and business rules (SBVR) is an adopted standard of the Object Management Group (OMG) containing business rules that was drafted and adopted in 2005 and published in 2008.

How And Why Business Rules Are Established

Business rules are established and monitored using the business rule guidelines when creating a business rule. Business rules are setup to help businesses achieve goals for failures in businesses because of poor strategies, inconsistent business practices, or unfulfilled business rules. Business rules must be implemented as a business requirement and form the basis of rules to help prepare system flows or procedural flow charts and provide an outline of a rule for the operation of a business. Business rules must highlight efficiency, consistency, predictability, and many other advantages and ensure that there are no failures for rules implemented and met. Business rules must meet expectations and guidelines on how work will be conducted by a business. Business rules are established to comply with local, state, and federal regulatory requirements and provide governance for a project. Business rules are established to address safety, and conflict resolution, reduce errors, and prevent litigation suits. Business rules identified in different areas of an organization must be met by different groups of people (managers, employees, customers, and others) in different roles for fulfillment of a rule.

CHAPTER 2

Need for Business Rules

According to (Mckinnon, 2019), businesses must avoid analysis-paralysis, delayed decision-making, and inaction due to prolonged over-analysis. Business rule improvement methodology is a continuous open-flow process model defined to meet rule customizations for improvements made in small increments to adhere to standards of a balanced and well-maintained application. Business rule success depends on process flow for tracking and creating business rules daily, extending business rule improvements to meet the business rule framework need, and revising rules for improvements and various others. Mckinnon cites that developing a routine for daily activities will save a lot of rule failures when a business grows. In the case of certain companies, business rules were not monitored as continuity rules for use as re-use rules or new revision rules. Third-Party systems maintained a set of business rules different from internal systems that showed discrepancies in business rule implementation causing differences in product order tracking and order reporting resulting in revenue differentials.

CHAPTER 3

How and why Business Rule Failures Occur

According to (Zorc, 2019), the top eight reasons why implementations fail are poor planning and miscommunication. Some of these include projects that are big where costs and process variants are too much to manage. Some factors list why business rule failures take place. There are no control monitors to monitor timeline or tools to track flows such as team skills expertise and rate of progression. Other implementation failures include, lack of communication, project management milestone failures, user acceptance testing, people resources, and time.

Lack of Preparation
System Implementations fail for lack of preparation such as, for example selection of new IT tools that did not meet the criteria of business rule requirement. The gaps in the system is not met because the system is not modified or supplemented to meet the business rule criteria.

De-prioritization of Tasks Not Prioritized
An implementation failure results when the staff is not committed, or implementation takes a back seat for other tasks, or a task is missed. Sometimes, a project lacks requirements for a feature set in one or two cycles and falls behind, and

the deadlines are postponed resulting in the de-prioritization of tasks.

Budget for plans not met: Implementations also fail because budgets for the plan are not scaled and not managed well, or budgets are based on time and materials. An example is spending excessively in a certain area of the project resulting in wastages with no return on investment.

Incompetency of skills: The project not meeting the needs of the project because of the new learning of a team on the job, or a lack of talent of a team to complete a project on time, or a new technology requiring new implementation expertise. IT implementations require precision and planning of a project and resource that can cause business failure.

Processes on the job not current: There are dysfunctions in the job processes such as accountability and commitment, because of poor preparation and project planning, causing abandonment of projects for business rule failures.

Management Not Establishing a Clear Schedule for Deliverables

There is a lack of commitment of an organization for a focus of politics rather than the need to meet deliverables. Over scaling a project and constant change modifications will cause implementation failures. The processes of business rule framework must be orchestrated through policy guidelines for correct implementation. Software development and implementation guidelines do not meet goals for fulfillment if there are no sprint iteration cycles mapped, product features defined, and team collaboration for team expertise skills not met for business needs.

According to (Talekar, 2017), business rules through digital transformation are not only tied to structured data but to unstructured data as well. Business rules generate patterns and actions, as new rules translating systems using business rule criteria defined. Digital transformation includes common business rule patterns such as eligibility patterns, val-

idation patterns, authority and approval patterns, calculation patterns, cognitive patterns, and others. Business rules
need to be defined through business rule patterns such as
validation patterns, verification patterns, map rule patterns,
and various others. Examples of business rule patterns are,
a validation pattern for an order submittal validating the
tax for a certain region vs other regions, a verification rule if
the order was completed through an order process flow for
an order channel, an order map rule for an order mapped
to a requirement such as if multiple products can be bought
for the same bundle.

According to (Ismail, 2019), 83% of global organizations
experienced third-party incidents such as loss of data,
hacking, theft and various others because of cyberattacks.
Business rule failures result in significant impairment of
customer service, material financial losses, reputational
damage, and regulatory breaches. Third-party systems
are not able to deliver products or protect customers for
business rule failures. The revenue losses from third-party
failures ranged for a company from £1.3 million to £35
million and increased to £650 million. The business rule
failures that emerged from this case example is point to a
failure of system because of lack of effective business rules
to track third-party systems, not providing remedial measures, creating a gap of system failure. Business rule failures point to lack of knowledge and training of customer
service representatives, when placing customer orders,
refunding orders, or understanding customer needs. CSR
Organizations have short-term and long-term impacts when
responding to quick changes, and potential risks, because
business rule failures are not robust, or not mapped to case
scenarios. Education Facts data contains data submitted by
SEAs, LEAs, and schools by DQ phases for submission and
Post submission categories. The data submitted by these
agencies contains errors and does not match the business

rule criteria measured through rule logic and rule formula. The rule criteria and rule logic must be matched based on the business rule data criteria for business rule fulfillment. Business rule mapping must have rule subsets based on union, intersect, query joins, and other computations to accommodate a case scenario either for a new improvement, maintenance, or for a new rule.

Business rule reliance without validation and verification for a case, or a test, results in system failure, because a system failure is not validated and verified for support through a business rule metric for a rule met. According to (Swami, 2020), data quality must be validated for the following types of data failures to prevent business rule failures:

Data Quality Intrinsic – Accuracy: The data defined must be reflected accurately. Examples of data accuracy include data defined for a customer placed order for a product such as order id, order status, customer name, and other order details.

Data Integrity: The data defined meets integrity criteria for data maintenance and data accuracy and consistency when stored in a database or when sent to a customer.

Data Validity: The data defined is stored in a specific format and follows business rule requirements and is in a format specified. An example of data validity is if the data met the unique key constraint and relational integrity constraint.

Data Accessibility: Accessibility, access security, is dependent upon data quantity and coverage for accuracy, reliability, and for data structured. An example of data accessibility is data that can be accessed after valid authentication and authorization.

Contextual: Contextual rules refer to rules for relevancy, timeliness, and completeness. The different views of a contextual representation are different from actual observation, not accounting to rules met for incompleteness, ambiguousness and meaningless representation, a contextual difference of an architectural perspective of system infrastructure and how it refines and improves data quality for time-based ecommerce perspectives such as if the B2B ecommerce closes a deal that may impact the data quality, connection of heterogeneous databases and others.

Representational: Rules refer to Consistency, conciseness, and interpretability of data. The data defined compares to and is the same as the data sent to the customer as a customer report and matches the data on a server. We can determine from these factors that the data quality is dependent on several factors that impact data for different validity criteria rules.

CHAPTER 4

Business Failures in different phases of software cycles

A failure pattern emerges when the system is in the extension phase and causes business rule failures. When the system is in the sustainment and maintenance phase, the architect must make a trade-off to add value to the system, and not accrue technical debt. The system does not payback on the original investment in the sustainment phase because the system becomes expensive and a goal to achieve long-term sustainment for a value to deliver, is an emphasis with little or no change to architecture or system. The same was the case when the educational facts data matured with little or no design changes going through failure patterns of sustainment and maintenance mode, causing the same number or more number of rule errors for system failures.

Business Failures for Mismatch of Skills and Roles

Failure patterns of an architect (IEEE software Column, 2016) result from a mismatch of skills and roles based on a need of time. The wrap around pattern is one where the architect is not a sustainer with no skills in current technologies but is well-versed in legacy systems. The rising star is a failure pattern where the developer steps into the role of an architect for profitable integration. The overprotective pattern is a failure pattern where the architect does both the initial phase and integration phase role, and the system does not deliver value to fulfill competitive growth. (Techbeacon, 2017) cited that some of the developer failures included deletion of a production database on the server because of running a script for a configuration rule in the production database.

Business Failures for Lack of Skills Acquisition

The role of a new developer must be defined to ensure safeguards are in practice when onboarding new developers (Codementor, 2017). Other failures included exposure of sensitive data on git-hub, a developer published source code that contained documents of five global financial institutions (Osakwe, 2020). The software configuration process was not built as part of control procedures causing business rule failures of these businesses. In this case, test user ids were used in production and test orders created, causing inaccurate order tracking and reporting for revenue calculation. Roles of developers and architects must be re-defined for on-time resolution of defects, for well-defined deployments, infrastructure efficiencies removing constraints on utilization and flexibility for access.

Point To Tracked Business Failures

An example of a point to track business failure is test cases for a system maintained by Dodge that did not cover all scenarios (Hatter, 2017), resulting in the recall of 1.25 million Dodge RAM pickup trucks due to a fatal bug in onboard computer software, that would have caused the driver to rollover. Another developer failure was the internal build pushed into production by the software team, a mistake where builds were sent only to the MS insider group. A software bug caused $280 million, inaccessible to cryptocurrency wallet holders (Chickowski, 2017). A bug allowed a user to gain access to several multi-signature wallets and deleted the code library that supported the wallets. Apple implemented an auto-correct feature that replaced "I" with an "A", and a Unicode question mark, causing issues for end-users. The article states that developers should not be the cause of single point of failures, and controls-based backstops must be put in place to prevent developer failure errors causing system failures (Browne, 2017). An example of a system is where the development team used incorrect coding practices, causing code errors resulting in business rule failures.

Quality Assurance (QA) Business Failures

A business improvement rule model must create a business rule map process flow for verification and validation result, a verification that business rules have been met. According to (Schlosser, 2020), data quality rules are business rules that define business requirements of data validation rules for the purpose intended. Data quality rules use measurement methods of data quality dimensions to meet the contextual accuracy of values for correctness and accuracy, consistency of values for format and completeness of values. Quality control measures allow for validation and verification of business rules met through QA for test cases of all business rule scenarios. Business rules for product validation and verification must be compared with standard benchmark metrics for proof of verification result. Examples of reporting business rules failures are shown in the Appendix section in Figure 5-8. (Examples include, 5-year edit failures, dropouts, CCD schools, Completeness – Digits in 4 years, Grades offered, Grade Completers, and others).

CHAPTER 5

An Analysis of Business Failures

According to (Priest, 2019), data-based decision-making is the approach to business rule success to backtrack negative revenue tracing for improved metric revenue growth and for good customer experience. Business rules must be validated and tagged for accuracy of revenue metrics. According to (Zhang, 2019), metrics innovation and challenges must be a creative measure to meet or exceed revenue metrics for business rule success.

An analysis of business rule failures with impact studies has been discussed in previous pages discussing the negative impact of business rules on education data failures. The study will identify business improvement rules to prevent business rule failures in a company. A Harvard Business Review article stated that agile teams for an organization are not a fit in all contexts and must be assessed for a given situation before implementation (Rigby, Sutherland & Noble et al., 2018). Other authors echoed the same opinion that a situation can be detrimental, whereas best practices in one. (Bock, 2015; Mueller-Hanson & Pulakos, 2018). The reasons for business rule failures of Education Facts Data are listed as follows: The submitted Supervisory Union ID for the SU or RESA was not unique within the state, The Zip Code Plus 4 for Mailing and/or Location Address is invalid, File submission included multiple rows of data for the same educational unit, Submitted State Assigned School or LEA Identifier is not found in EDEN, School or Agency is not operational, and a dropout count was reported, Inconsistent Dropout Reporting: Sum of dropouts by grade (Subtotal 1) does not equal the grand total (EUT), LEA dropout submission does not include all applicable, offered grades, Mailing and/or location address is not provided in Directory submission and others.

CHAPTER 6

Business Rule Best Practices

An organization must chart a competitive path by reallocating resources through organizational agility from sensing and redirection to build new capabilities where no value is generated (Worley et al., 2014). A system must use a product development open-continuous model for re-utilization of user stories, value determination of user stories, scarcity usage scenarios, revised requirements criteria approach, conditional fulfillment criteria, partial fulfillment criteria, rethink scenarios, and others.

Business rules must be tagged (A business rule metric met must be set to a status of verified for a business rule met in the database) for every business rule success or failure, a measure of a business rule improvement indicator. Steve Jobs changed the strategy of a ``Consumer" and "Pro" and the rows of "Desktop" and "Portable." to a new strategy for a brand of simplicity to help customers understand the products and services of Apple (Isaacson, 2011). Business rules in systems must be measured through KPI indicators based on growth strategies in all areas of business operations. A company had a negative revenue loss of $500.00 per month for a customer order category per customer, and the revenue loss was not measured through metrics using lean revision studies for business improvement. The negative impact scenarios are not measured for business rule failures for systems re-evaluated for growth through value-added categories for requirements re-utilization category, code re-utilization category, defect re-utilization category, release re-utilization category and others. Organizations leveraged networked teams to connect seamlessly using organizational culture for transformation of business success (Deloitte, 2017). Companies are leveraging team partnerships strategies by driving teamwork and collaboration to support these new structures to launch new competencies, expectations, and training (Edmondson, 2018). New business case scenarios such as keyword mapping, test or other map flows was not identified for the Education Data Single Inventory System. New knowledge acquisitions for innovation to launch new product technologies was limited for the application.

Roles and Responsibilities of IT
Software Engineering (Chicowski, 2017) cites three roles and three software patterns for system failures (Klein, 2016). The software architect must have knowledge and training in technologies for system integration, such as middleware, application programming interface (APIs), or communications protocol. The architect must be a member of the initial development team and understand the capabilities of a system documented and undocumented from the start.

CHAPTER 7

Business Failure Examples

The research topic cites specific case examples of research, peer and journal articles as well as online newspaper articles to augment specific cases of business rule failures.

Software Company Security Bug
A software company defined business rules at different stages of software implementation to detect software security bugs. This business rule was defined for integrity of customer data, userid, password and others stored in the database. This business rule failed, and the data stolen and misused by a third party.

Software Security Breach
A software company encountered security breach via remote access that provided access to customer data. A user posted the user authentication code on the message boards on twitter for use by other parties. The hacking was exposed by a twitter group, and the customers of third-party companies brought accusations against the software company.

Covid-19 Failures
The impact (Shahroz, Ahmad & et al., 2021) of COVID-19 pandemic has negatively impacted human mobility patterns such as the daily transportation-related behavior of

the public and set open challenges such as scalability, privacy, adaptability and highlighting promising directions for future work. In this case scenario, business rule failures did not identify the different categories of process rule failures such as failures for a situation of a covid-19 failure, failure for an algorithm not applied to a case scenario of covid-19, and the ripple effect of covid-19 for cases such as absence at work, low productivity, funding based on prioritization and others. An example of a covid-19 failure is the settings algorithm for a covid-19 application not updated after the initial software release. Another example of the business rule failure is not tracking a business rule to the latest patches, a document repository of business rules tracked to the most current (with metrics, 2020), an example of a company measured in terms of power, performance, and functionality through rule metrics.

Encryption Business Rule Software Failure
According to (Rust, 2020), a business rule failure was the client software that enabled a remote hacker to control a PC running Windows 7 or earlier. The company did not have an end-to-end encryption software for user logins and allowed other meeting attendees to view user accounts and details such as user profiles, loginid and password details, and other types of hacking practices. This enabled other users to enter meetings, post and steal contents of meetings hosted by other users. The business rule failure of the software company points to failure of a two-factor authentication that must protection user accounts.

Data Security
A data security breach of a software company, a change made to the database network security group, contained misconfigured security rules that resulted in the exposure of data such as email addresses, IP addresses, and other data exposures of the system. Another example is a software company that had a huge data breach and exposed 268

million customer records that contained personal information such as names and usernames, email and IP addresses, genders, general geographic location, birth dates, and passwords stored as bcrypt hashes.

Software Implementation Business Failures

Numerous examples abound that reveal how a data security rule failed. (A violation of user encryption not to expose user records) that caused a business rule failure (Cigniti, 2020). The software Company confirmed a data breach that exposed 500 million user credentials, showing a lack of user security rules to protect system data causing system failures. The information stolen from the company's network in 2014 included names, email addresses, telephone numbers, dates of birth, hashed passwords (the vast majority with bcrypt), and in some cases, encrypted or unencrypted security questions and answers.

CHAPTER 8

Software Business Failures

Software updates for a thermostat contained product bugs where users could not heat their homes or use amenities. The product bug caused drainage of the battery of thermostats and deactivated the system. The customers complained of cold temperatures because of a non-functional thermostat. The failure in the product is a business rule that did not meet the criteria of standards of quality for failure of a product rule.

Business Rule Failures
The business rule failures of a system that failed to process 275,000 individual payments left people without pay before a bank weekend holiday. This was termed by a UK bank as an isolated issue, a business rule that was missed or skipped and was not included as part of the business rule framework. Business rule failures were also due to product catalog match failures of vendor product rules defined for systems, and that did not match internal system rules.

Implementation Failures
According to Accounting Seed Firm, the U.S Navy lost over $ 1 billion in the implementation failure of four ERP systems. The costs and variables involved in the massive projects were just too much to manage, resulting in busi-

ness rule failures because of deficient system features not matching business requirements. Business rule failures in IT implementation were also because of a few moderate to low levels of employee skills not matching the required technical skills for a job, causing failure of roles and responsibilities.

Data Quality Failures

An example of data quality failure is customer orders placed inaccurately, or customer orders not mapped correctly for validation and population of the database. Business rule failures for lack of test rule criteria include software configuration test failures. According to (Knowledgebase, 2017), the A400M airbus experienced a quality issue in parts of the flying machine. The failure was not in the code but in the design settings of the current electronic unit of the motors. Nissan recalled a million vehicles, as the front passenger-side airbag was not deployed in a crash. Honda Motors recalled 104,871 vehicles, as the airbag was deemed faulty by journalists. A programming error was identified as the cause of the alarm failure and the reason behind the Northeast blackout. Software security bugs were detected in OLA mobile app, taxi services in India. OLA tried to fix bugs, but there were bugs in the operating system.

Software Defect Failures

According to (Vyaas, 2020) software defects cannot be prevented but must be communicated responsibly. Software defect management process must meet business rule requirements through business rule improvement measures for business rule fulfillment. Defect resolution is not utilized using optimal code policy standards. There is a wide gap between business flow processes and system implementation processes in all phases of system development life cycle derived from poor business rules and a non-robust business rule framework methodology. (Dexcom, 2020), could not identify the root cause of business failures when there was a server overload that generated a massive backlog, and the company was unable to pin down the underlying problem. There were deployment release failures when code was deployed referencing the wrong code in the repository and added to the defects list. Several research articles have been published, citing examples of business failures, but no study was undertaken to augment multiple business scenarios that caused business rule failures.

CHAPTER 9

Mitigation of Business Failures

According to (Priest, 2019), businesses must build business cases successfully to avoid business rule failures. Businesses cannot cite causes as business rule failures but must find predictive accuracy to allow for business rule success through expertise and rigorous evidence. Business rule failures can be prevented through database decision-making rules and system automation rules for a better customer experience. Business leaders must have a focus on reenergizing people and organizations to build on failures during crisis times and to reexamine the identity of an organization for continued growth. Leaders have identified a trend for increased connectivity, lower transaction costs, increased automation and a shift in demographics (Mckinsey, 2021). Another area where organizations must succeed for business success is in researching new and key solutions in areas such as customer and product fulfillment for business solutions to replace business failures (Marcus Business Team, 2019). Some companies reinvented their businesses using new inventions and innovative approaches to increase and promote growth. An example is Amazon which targeted growth by establishing an e-commerce and cloud computing platform to increase revenue sales and increase customer growth in different areas of business through diversification strategies for business success. American Express reinvented its business through offering a charge card that extended credit to consumers and businesses. The company issued 110 million credit cards and 55 million cards to the US company Chipotle that reinvented its business using drive-thru pickup lanes that it calls chipotle lanes where more customers were served in a short amount of time avoiding the long lines of delay (US Chamber of Commerce, 2020) and promoting growth for business low and business errors. Test improvement rules must be included as part of business rule framework for any software development change or for rule changes configured as part of business rule revision. A test of business rules must expose situations for an impact on customer experience, such as when a customer places an order, the order flow from order placement to order fulfillment must be tracked easily by a customer for order fulfillment to customer order history. Test cases for system tests are done with no business rule model methodology, renewing defect failures, and losing business rule premise.

According to Bean and Davenport (2019), achieving data transformation, competing business on analytics, and managing data successfully in all its forms is a prerequisite of business rule success. Data rules are mapped incorrectly to data models, impacting company revenue, and system data map failures. An example is a data rule not mapped correctly to different regions causing inaccurate reporting and data inaccuracy. Another example is business rules that do not include cases of configuration setup for a code deployment rule.

Mitigation for a Business Rule Integrity Model

According to (Hulu et al., 2020), cross-validation empiricism results in data accuracy for similarity in the proximity of a measurement result compared to the actual number. Cross-validation is used as a measure of test-criteria based on the accuracy of test data parameters specified by cross-validation business improvement rule and cross-validation data failure rules for business integrity rule fulfillment. Cross-validation helps to validate and verify metrics for the before and after state (with the new data) for business rule accuracy fulfillment. A negative business metric must be revised through a benchmark revision of business rule for improvement.

CHAPTER 10

Summary

According to (Edubirdie, 2020), a summary provides an overview of the study and preserves the structure and sections of the article it focuses on. Chapter 2 discussed literature review to support studies for business rule failures through a definition of business rules, and a discussion of literature review by expounding and synthesizing other research studies to support the current study. The impact of business rule failures have been defined using the different sub-headings such as business rule definition, origin of business rules, how and why business rules are established, business failures in different phases of software cycle, citation of business failure examples, business rule tagging for validation and verification checks, business rule failure impacts, study framework hypothesis, and business rules overflow contained through accurate product validity and verification model and others.

Chapter 11

Business Rule Failure Recommendations

According to (Pensters, 2016), recommendations are a way to suggest measures for resolution of issues to benefit a study. Recommendations are based on data and other measures and must be justified with empiricism using proof of support. Please see below my recommendations for the study of business rule failures.

Other business rule recommendations must be implemented using a small sample study for improved growth scenarios defined in the following cases:

Business Improvement Map Rules:
Business rule failures must be mapped to one or more improvement rules for business rule fulfillment. These map rules must include keyword or key phrase association for map to a business rule using either code flow map rule, test flow map or other flows.

Test Rule Map:
Test rule failure must be mapped to business improvement rules for impact scenarios such as revenue loss, product failure, test accounts used in production, and others. Example: A test failure flow must be mapped to a business improvement code/test flow through validation and verification flows for a business rule for fulfilment.

Code Rule Map:

Code failure rules must be mapped to business improvement rules for impact scenarios such as for code skipped, code isolated, code not augmented, code referencing a different version of code and various others. An example is a code failure flow map to a business improvement rule for a rule applied for a few conditions, and skipping others, is a code flow rule for use or re-use for every business rule criteria defined.

Keyword Rule Map:

A new keyword rule identified by a customer must be used to relate the flow for different areas of a requirement flow. Key words with synonyms for business rules met must be understood and related to the business rule.

Customer Service Training Rules: Customer Service Agent training rules must be mapped for different CSR rule flows to fulfill customer expectations. Customer service agent training flows must include business rule flows for product order flows, customer placement of orders, customer subscription and product renewals and various others for business rule fulfillment.

Vendor Training Rules: Vendor training rules must be mapped using keyword association for new product flows, and update of existing flows for business rule fulfilment. Vendor rules must use new rules for product growth using new knowledge process flows in products to fulfill customer expectations.

Customer Training Rules: Customer training rules must be mapped to new and existing flows for order placement, shopping cart rules, subscription rules for membership and others A commitment to commit to a date is only true for a delivery met for a business rule fulfilled. A commitment to product delivery met for a vendor flow is for a feature, new or old with no delay or latency of time, decision, or revenue loss for a positive business value earned for a business rule fulfilled.

CHAPTER 12

Suggestions for Future Research

Data Augmentation Studies:
Combined critique business rules method: A critique of business rules combined and translated into new business rules for new growth or failure scenarios.
Points to synonyms method: A requirement of a business rule translated to a synonym point met for a business rule fulfilled.
Ivy Curve Method: Extension business rules that belong to one or more abstraction classes for business rule fulfillment.
New Paradigms to be included:

- Business rule framework must include new paradigms (theories), elaborated through scientific research methodologies such as point to synonyms met method for a business rule(s) met (DMadiraju, 2021).

- Business rule solution methods must include individual data scenarios for a difference(s) of comparison with other data records, to identify discrepancies in data records and evaluate solutions through new solutions for new business improvement rules.

- Business rule framework must use data revision studies using new data filter sets to provide new data intelligence studies for analysis from artificial intelligence and other scientific intelligence systems.

- Business rules for data encapsulation must be leveraged through metaphors from diverse components of quality data to include meaningful interpretation of data for a business rule validity.

- Business rule framework for data structures must create data patterns using metaphors that describe an aspect of a study for a value of a difference. This can resemble a business rule pattern for a definition of a similarity or a difference for a defect pattern rule.

- Business rule definition interpretation must identify uncertainties to situations, conditions for fulfillment, decision latency, implementation for a factor such as scarcity of a need or utilization through util measures (based on estimates) to verify business rule accuracy to interpret results.

Data Segmentation Studies:

Parallel Business Rules: A leaf study with lines across will have parallel rules for two sets of studies for a difference, or for a similarity.

Onion studies Business Rules: Each layer is a new core business rule inner layer and is needed to fulfill a business rule.

Several ivy curve maps for a business rule: A result derived from several business rule maps. A dependency rule is extended to derive or create a business rule and is part of a complete rule for several rules.

CHAPTER 13

Concluding the Study

According to (Bouchrika, 2021), conclusion is a summary of the introduction, and body of the paper. The author identified the root cause of business rule failures and suggested business rule improvement measures for business growth. Comparison studies from industry sources were cited through journals, government studies, corporate, and other websites to identify the number of business rule failure occurrences for different business failure categories.

The author identified new improvement measures for business rule failures based on data studies, and data scenarios, and provided new ways to analyze data to map rules for calculation metric data using utilization theory of incremental value to add value to a product. The author provided suggestions to identify new business improvement(s) rules using future value stream map of value generation processes using decision-based case model, artificial intelligence techniques and hybrid map models based on data, and algorithm for business rule accuracy.

The author concludes the study by stating that business rule failures happen in any area of business and must be tracked, monitored and eliminated using business improvement rules. Solutions for business rule failures must be identified based on growth strategies using case study examples, knowledgebase studies, collaboration solutions with external and internal vendors, strategic partnerships with organizations, new knowledge acquisitions, new innovation and invention studies all based on business rule acceptance criteria defined through business rule solutions paradigm.

The author concludes the study with a message to everyone that business rule failures are a part of any a process and must be tested using a unit for a complete test measurement method. A rule must be tested using a measure such as a rule created is equal to a rule met for a result, such as for an addition for a number added, a subtraction for a number subtracted or others. The rule must shown as a mathematical or statistical metric for a business rule fulfillment.,A complex rule must be created based on paradigm implementation of several solutions and solutions chosen based on rule criteria met for process flow for a result value implementation. The rule criteria can be proved using a graph or a linear equation for a solution approach. New graphs and new types of equations can also be used based on information extracted for a business requirement for business rule fulfillment.

Part 2: Business Intelligence Theories

Chapter 1

Business Corner Theory

Business corners is a concept where a business has corners of wastages in areas of business not utilized effectively, a business value not realized in a corner of a business. These business corners denote loss of revenue harvest in business corners such as, a building value unutilized, revenue value not accounted for, a goodwill value not visible and lost, and a short gain I acquired (purchase of) only for a purpose wasted, a business corner revenue not realized and wasted for a business purpose misaligned.

A business corner can be defined using active or passive constructors for past, present or future occurrences with reference to a period of time, a season, a time, a value metric not tracked. A piece of land outside my home is a land I own that has been unutilized and is not shown in the balance sheet for any a value. An intangible asset such as a knowledge I acquired by listening to a seminar has not been utilized in my work or a productivity gain not utilized and caused a corner not utlilized fully.

Business corner methods for a business must be calculated based on a equation for a wastage. A business corner value can also be calculated using an angle to compute a wastage. A right, left corner, Obtuse,Acute, and other angles for wastages. These rules must be tested with hypothesis based on business rule criteria for a negation vs alternative approaches.

Business Corners Lost

1. Product created and not sold.

There are no orders placed by a customer(s). There is no revenue from such a corner, and these corners are wasted. These need to be identified using slim approach improvements practice.

2. An installation service was done at the customer site, but the revenue was not accounted for. A business corner of a revenue wasted and business corners not accounted for using the slim improvement practices.

3. Subscription fees were duplicated for a customer increasing the revenue from an unaccounted category. Such a data corner is a business corner showing wrong revenue for accountability and is a hidden revenue loss, called hidden business value not created for a revenue value accrued.

4. Renewal of Customer subscription fees for a service was not collected and accounted for in the report, showing a business corner wrong from an accounting and reporting perspective of a business corner.

5. A business corner I need to gain must be created with a boundary limit for a set of business values defined for a business strategy showing a gain and a business corner advantage.

6. Vendor training manuals must be updated so that vendors can help customer place orders using the right procedures.

7. Duplicate report maintenance on the vendor and internal vendors creates mismatch of report totals, a busi-

ness corner, lost when matching revenue corners for a balance.

8. A left business corner is a product limited by a product lean on a business corner of a competitor to generate a business value.

9. A translation of a product into a different type or a service is a loss of a business corner lost for a value of a plain vs a plaid or a formal vs an informal lost, a value not fully realized.

10. A crevice in a product is a loss of a product value for a business corner lost. A crevice is a faulty product, a value that did not match when I saw the product and ordered online, only to move away to a new product on a new product website.

CHAPTER 2

Data Harvest Theory

How do we grow data (revenue corner) lost for a business corner failure.

Open Data Theory concept:

A Business rule strategy for a data set already used at a certain value must be combined using the dataset for other strategies not to lose data value. Data Value is to re-use the same, add or subtract (a slight deviation) for a data value gain. We need to organize data corners for a business value earned. Amaximization of a business corner value is to examine the business corners wasted (value realizers) and add value corners to the business using data value corners. These business corners must be reviewed using a chart or an excel sheet such as a leaf chart, showing crevices for data corners lost, or an ivy curve chart for imperfections for value corners gained. This is called theory of data harvest gain for a business corner lost.

We need to research, define and aggregate the collective values of customers and create business rules around these values to reduce waste using a culture of responsibility, repair and reuse to improve customer base and for long-term customer relationships(Harvard Business Review, 2016).

CHAPTER 3

Data Corner Theories

Custom Data Theory:
A custom data theory concept is a definition of a dataset used to create several data strategies, to create a custom dataset for a business value. This dataset is a custom dataset used for several purposes to earn business value.

Closed Data Theory
A set of data not useful and does not generate data value is categorized as data wasted and not effectively used. It is a type of data strategy used to avoid revenue loss for a price value and a product offering not for purchase by a consumer.

A straight line business corner theory: is defined as a business corner theory that uses a business corner rule or formula for a single set of data combination to generate data value based on a business strategy of a fixed value to generate for business revenue.

A Sum Balance Business Corner Theory
A sum balance business corner theory is a theory where all corners of a business add to a total sum, for a business sum value balanced.

Chapter 4

Business Depreciation Corner Theories

Business Corner Depreciated Theory: A data period is assigned for review and evaluation of a business loss of a business corner based on a dataset compared from a straight line to a percentage or a point depreciated corner value. The business corner is compared to an appreciated value of a business corner for a period from base to a percentage increase every month until the end of the business season. Business Rule Balance for a business revenue corner gained theory A business rule balance is a business corner balanced of a corner gained by matching the value corner of a business with an equal or more value translated in the same or another area.

Angled Business Corner Theory
All angles of a business corner are translated through business corner equations for a balance such as an angle for a sum value, an angle for a depreciated or appreciated value and others.

Business Crack Theory
A business crack theory is a theory where a crack in a business is either visible or invisible and the crack is traced for repair and maintenance to repaired and maintained for a business to continue or exist.

A Business Corner Definition for Business Ambiguity theory

A business corner ambiguity must be deleted for a wastage or defined clearly for a business objective fulfilment accomplished.

CHAPTER 5

Business Requirement Solutions Digest

A business requirement digest must cover all areas of business wastages and deficiencies to effective business corners gained. The requirements digest must show solutions completed with success using a business requirement method for a business corner, a business flat surface, a business crevice and others for a business requirement solution. These business requirements methods fall under the following categories:

- A New business requirement for a business corner wasted identified for a use.

- An existing business requirement, a wastage or deficiency in the form of a crevice not for use, or a use must be identified and solution identified in the requirements digest.

- A business acquired for a purpose to generate revenue, and has edges, corners and crevices needs to be identified in the requirements solutions digest.

- A business requirement(s) wasted, deficient, does not show a value, a maintenance cost high with the same value every year, and a unidentified cost not visible must be identified in the requirements solutions digest.

- A business requirement not a need, but a luxury item that does not generate use to drive sales, a consumer tool manual and does not generate a new thinking or rethink for a new sales generation technique must be identified with solutions in the requirements solution digest.

- A business requirement archived with all scenarios must be reviewed for new solutions using new scenarios in the requirements solutions digest.

CHAPTER 6

Business Corner Symmetry Theory

Business Corner Symmetry theory is a symmetry of how many ways can we save and balance a business corner. We need to research and define the collective values of customers and create business rules (Harvard Business Review) around these values to reduce waste using a culture of responsibility, repair and reuse to improve customer base for long-term customer relationships.

All business corners must be reviewed for symmetry based on measures implemented and measured for accuracy of a balanced corner. Some business corners to review include, corners with a fold, a corner not clear and faded, a corner not matching the shape for a symmetry and to be re-matched using solutions to match the shape for a geometric business corner. These solutions must be accurate to meet the criteria of a business corner save and balance a business for business existence, growth, and regeneration.

A business corner with a fold may include costs not used economically, wastages in production called defects, products sold and deemed as a business corner fold. A business corner fold must be ironed out in all areas of business such as product requirements, product input for process, product finish using QA standards for met, and other criteria to smooth a fold before a product implementation for a business symmetry met. A business corner fold can be in any area of a product cycle and must be ironed out in each area with geometric measure solutions for a smooth product finish to customer fulfillment to business corner symmetry.

A business corner symmetry must be defined using criteria inputs for all possible corner scenario folds and measured using a filter to match a solution (s) for a rule criteria corner to a symmetry. A business corner symmetry is a symmetry balance of all four corners of a business to embody the concept of pillar of strength for a balance of business corner symmetry.

A business owner does not look at the business corners for a balance, but looks at the volume of business, sales revenue and profit margin. A business corner fold may be invisible and hidden and is a liability, and misses a good will value for a business symmetry. The hidden liability asset cannot be balanced in the balance sheet and continues to accumulate and grow as a debt hidden until visible. These liability business corners must be traced and tracked every year from the time a business comes into existence, and shown as a liability in the balance sheet. A depreciated value factor must be set aside as reserves for a liability of a business corner wasted and not balanced as a business symmetry. A business corner assymetry will be balanced and the business corner folds smooth provided the solution criteria details are implemented to match the business corners for a symmetry. The solutions not matched and wasted are shown as liability factors and must be eliminated every year for a symmetry.

CHAPTER 7

Business De-Stress factor Theory

Business Destress can be defined as business processes failing due to factors such as efforts not tracked in different areas of business to accumulate failure factors as stress factors. These business cases must be reevaluated by a business expert to trace business case scenarios to identify factors that cause a stress for a failure scenario. This happens in areas where a stress factor exists and these factors cause failures in business processes hindering business growth. Business stress factors are linked to different business case failure scenarios. Each destress factor is a link in a value chain business process identified for a stress factor. The business destress factors must be tracked and validated for each effort for verification to a success path in a value stream process. The effort must be translated to learning values based on the effort researched for a positive outcome for success.

Business value scenario failures must be translated to de-stress linked scenarios:

The business destress factors must be tracked using the path of reasons paradigm to identify the correct destress factor causing business failures. These factors must be categorized and de-stress factors identified for a single or multiple de-stress factors.

The following are the key de-stress factors that need to be tracked through de-stress factor identifiers.

- Failures from learning (Harvard Business Review, 2011). The managers and their teams were not able to provide effective solutions to bridge the gaps in failures even after a learning of a problem. They were thinking the failures the wrong way and the efforts led to no change.

- Failures from existing efforts that cause stress factors.

- Failures from research failed for no solutions.

- Failures from ineffective participant skills to delivery theory

- Problem based solution action theory to identify a destress factor for effective problem resolution.

- Learning for effective action theory through a review of stress factors using examples of case scenarios to destress for a problem solution.

CHAPTER 8

Business Edge Theory

A business edge I need to be careful about is for a business period that did not factor an edge for a value lost based on a single occurrence of a business parameter, an edge I lost for not knowing the competitor market factor based on a dynamic price key factor and others. Please see below the price paradigms.

Price Paradigm Theory
A business can generate revenue and minimize costs based on different pricing strategies.
Price based on a few Paradigms:

1. Select a few products based on price points (low or high) to generate revenue.

2. Price based on culture.

3. Price based on a set number of customers.

4. Price based on length of a sale or a measure met for a sale.

5. Price based on family-derived metrics.

6. Price based on average sale for product(s).

7. Price combined for a composite value.

8. Price based on different price pattern sets.

9. Price based on geometrically calculated values for optimal price-product value.

10. Price based on a ceiling limit restricted for reasons such as consumer spending, limited capital, product type such as economic or luxury based goods.

CHAPTER 9

Lean Cost Business Strategy Theory

A Lean Cost Theory can be defined as a cost theory that must use a liability based cost differentiation model for each category of cost wastage, cost aggregation over time, cost filter of inputs, process and output, cost quotients that are invisible, and cost determination for a new time period.

Cost structure can be categorized into different forms such as for a structure created based on pricing paradigms as well as on cost comparison critique of current to future value methods, or new cost setting criteria based on cost effective models using different categories of wastages such as wastages to be factored, no wastage, efficiency of inputs used in different phases of product creation to implementation, time factor applied in different categories of product creation, and cost quotients that aggregate to a number must use a different set of formula to use the wastage rule.

CHAPTER 10

Business Distribution Variance Theories

A business distribution variance theory is a theory based on a business distribution cost variance factor(s) not using a slim measure distribution channel approach for different categories of business categories. The different phases in distribution must include factors for measures that are precise to identify variances for wastages or variances for a requirement for a need of a distribution process to avoid the variances.

An effective business distribution channel utilizes the principles of economic balance factors, for negative cost variance, excess cost variance for a base model, a cost variance that generates and controls excessive spending, cost variance for an imbalance based on location, situation, price, process flow, output metrics and other factors.

Business distribution channels must be created based on different types of business distribution patterns such as if there is a dependency of a business on others in product creation or if the price of a product is impacted negatively based on product price combination patterns in different stages of product creation.

A few distribution variance theories are listed below:

- A distribution variance positive value based on cost value structure

- A distribution variance positive value based on price patterns creating a positive impact.

- A distribution variance comparison positive value based on cumulative value vs a segmented value for each segment of business.

- A distribution variance positive value based on economic value for a business value vs a non-lean cost approach

- A distribution variance saving value in different areas of business based on estimate comparisons using different types of algorithmic calculators for a distribution variance type.

Business channels must be created using focused differentiation strategies based on gains derived from each differentiation strategy such as for a competitive strategy, core strategy, Benefits vs risks strategy, growth strategy, distribution strategy and others.

CHAPTER 11

Business Distinct Culture Theory

A business distinct culture is a culture defined and met for business growth using business harmony and business peace factors for a business balanced earned value in all areas of business.

Business Distinct Culture
1. A culture based on the business origin, history or heritage values of business owner for a strategy based on family or other values

2. A culture based on a strategy shape that is shaped using different growth patterns such as a leaf pattern, a flower pattern, a branch and other patterns.

3. A culture using mathematical estimates to arrive at a business strategy solution. A mathematical formula such as an estimate using a linear equation, a statistical computation to arrive at a result for a business value earned.

4. A culture based on a paradigm(s) of business features such as variables to create a strategy pattern for a business value to earn.

5. A culture based on a walk of a season such as a purse, an autumn vs a summer is a seasonal strategy.

6. A culture to include different expressions, actions, and gestures, a customer requirement (that does not include verbal communication).

7. A culture based on conversational patterns, conversational abstracts, or conversational cases for a business strategy creation.

8. A culture based on a saving method vs an expense method to create conservative or expense business strategies.

9. A culture using a hidden investment pattern such as templates generation for a business purpose value to generate a business distinct culture.

10. A culture to create a business value for a business purpose using a custom criteria to generate an accrued value.

CHAPTER 12

Business Capable Conformity
Met Theory

A Business Capable Conformity concept is a theory where a business is capable of meeting standards of business to conformity for business existence to business growth to generate business value from business goals fulfilled. The business conformity definition also applies to a definition of conformity for business diversification to imply business growth for business capable conformity met. A business uncertainty factor is not visible for a business-capable conformity strategy implemented.

- A business capable conformity theory must adhere to the following business principles to meet business capable conformity standards:

- A business capable conformity for standards that match business standards defined for a business to generate revenue.

- A business capable conformity matches or is an alternative solution for a business capable conformity supported through verification of audited reports.

- A business capable conformity with risk and contingency solutions extending to new solution approaches for all scenarios supported through verified contingency documents.

- A business capable conformity standard approach that uses a single or multiple business strategies showing conformity for a business capable met through verified business value accrued and used.

- A business capable conformity met can also extend to a business capable conformity for a future value through estimation of sales revenue against previous financial statements for positive revenue, cost and profit margin.

- A business capable conformity met is a term used for a business capable of business continuity defined for a definite period and includes a balanced value of all assets and liabilities showing a positive number for a business value.

- A business capable conformity met is a value calculated using a function of price, demand, supply, and other inflationary factors to obtain a linear equation to determine a business capable conformity standard met using a graph value for a business value earned.

- A business capable conformity standard met is an accumulated value of business to growth using different set of equations for marketing, sales, economic, financial to growth.

Chapter 13

Business Dedicated for a Purpose Theory

A business dedicated concept is a business dedicated for a purpose to accomplish a business goal(s). A business dedicated purpose term is associated with a primary objective or goal fulfillment for a business dedicated to the goal or objective. A business dedicated is not for a commitment to a goal dedicated, but a commitment for a goal dedicated and fulfilled. A delivery of a goal fulfilled is a difference of a business dedicated for a business purpose to a commitment. A business dedicated for a purpose must match the following criteria to meet the definition of a business dedicated for a purpose.

- The objective of the business must be defined to match a business goal or criteria achieved for a business dedicated for a purpose. For example, a business dedicated for a business goal of fulfilling customer orders for a product(s) is a difference of the business diversifying into several areas of business producing different types of products, a difference of a goal committed to a delivery.

- A business dedicated must be defined separately as a different goal for a business dedicated for each business category and the goal commitment and fulfillment differs for each category of a business dedicated for a purpose of fulfillment or a fulfilled purpose.

- A business dedicated strategy for a purpose must match an outline for a goal defined for a business dedicated purpose. These strategies can fall under different areas of business alignment such as marketing, finance, customer, and other areas of business.

- A business dedicated must create dedicated boundaries for a business purpose. The boundaries define the limit for operating within the business precinct for a business dedicated for a business goal defined and fulfilled for a purpose.

- A business dedicated must define a business purpose for a transition state of a business, with a time period specified for a business dedicated and committed for a business goal fulfillment to fulfilled.

- A business dedicated for a purpose, must be defined using words such for, with, and (for addedndum), for clear specification for business goal commitment to fulfillment.

- A business dedicated for a purpose must define if single or multiple lines or channels of business dedicated for a same or a different purpose for goal fulfillment.

- A business dedicated for a purpose must state explicitly, and not be hidden for an implicit, the underlying cause(s) or a reason for not able to fulfill a business goal for a business dedicated for a business purpose.

- A business dedicated for a purpose must identify the factors that help a business grow for a time period for goal fulfillment as additional support factors for growth. These factors need to be clearly defined specifying the parameters such as time period, number, volume, revenue, demand, supply, tax and other factors. A linear equation using an econometric model can be used to justify the factors for estimation of growth for a business dedicated for a purpose of business growth to fulfillment. A tool such as an excel or other tools can be used for the purpose to justify the reasons for a business dedicated for growth to fulfillment.

- A business dedicated for a business purpose must define all the inputs and process flow that are used to complete a business purpose for fulfillment. Each input must define the reason(s) for a business dedicated for a purpose of growth. These inputs can changed based on new technology, skill, product type and the purpose must be revised for a business dedicated for a purpose for fulfillment. These serve as business detail strategies for different types of business inputs such as product sku, product category types, item detail types and others.

- A business dedicated for a purpose must define business strategies targeted for a business purpose using strategies based on price, cost, demand, supply, and others for a business dedicated for a purpose to fulfillment.

CHAPTER 14

Business Eloquent and Business Elegant Theory

Business Eloquence and Business elegance is a definition coined for a business growth of a business savvy, business sophisticate, a success, a brand for business growth. A business savvy purpose is a purpose met using different types of business savvy approaches for customer retention and customer growth.

Business terms elegant and eloquence are synonymous with a brand name and a brand image that a business associates with, such as a line of product, a luxury item, a brand association with a vendor business (that has a better reputation) and is business savvy using a different style, color, shape, and purpose to attract a customer(s). A business growth and a business continuity of a business is associated with a business synonym of a business elegance and business eloquence of a business only if it meets and exceeds the growth of revenue sales and creates a line of business as a luxury brand using a business savvy definition for the purpose of a business brand to highlight a business performing and exceeding business growth.

Business elegant and business eloquence are terms that can be combined using different strategies. These strategies must be clearly defined for a product(s) meeting the need(s) of a customer. These products can include products for a need, a luxury, or a customer(s) only comparing with customers to purchase the same product or a different product, a customer that wants a unique product or others. These products need to be created for a product quality, a product finish, a product image identified in product brochures to appeal to a customer(s) taste.

The terms business elegance and business eloquence also imply a business purpose for a type of product use to not only meet the basic needs of a customer, but also to extend the product use to different purposes. The product criteria is based on needs extending to new product types for a product savvy.

Business elegant and business eloquence is defined for a business purpose to emphasize the presence of business in the business world to attract customer presence for customer savvy for a product savvy to generate customer and product value. A company can be in several lines of business and also spell elegance and savvy in the way they dress, talk, behave and grace for a business value to generate.

Chapter 15

Business Generation Paradigm

A Business generation paradigm is a paradigm generated from every day business occurrences through meetings, interviews, and others to accrue business value for use in business improvement or growth scenarios, and is deemed effective business solutions.

- A business research filter for operators such as : € ^, |, + to create a new business generation category, a business value generated.

- A business hypothesis for a null and and an alternative to prove a new business generation proof of concept for a failure or for an alternative solution approach.

- A business exploratory research criteria based on data created for a research criteria to identify new topics of research for new business generation ideas.

- A business generation paradigm such as a focus to create a segment of a business using different research constructs to define business strategies outlining new business value methods for business growth is called a business segment focus for a new value earned paradigm.

- A business generation paradigm using a business harvest scenario to create a trend chart to focus on a product(s) generating revenue and to obtain new scenarios for new or existing value is a path of a new business value to grow of a business generated paradigm.

- A business generation paradigm using a combo product technique to generate revenue and re-generate value using cross business generation techniques is a business value generated for business growth.

- A business creative technique using existing data scenarios to create new data scenarios for different sets of customers and exchange the new data revised techniques in a circular quadrant fashion for a business purpose new or similar.

- A business generation paradigm technique to identify rows with max sales orders to create a subset of these orders using new price paradigm techniques to help business generate growth.

- A business cause or a business reason not generating revenue must be revised with new reasons and causes to create a revenue effect for business growth.

- A business generation method to create a business slice across several areas of business and to put together a new business value generated for business growth.

- A business accumulating loss in several areas and not creating business value, must create a business value through generating a new business purpose with a set of value strategies targeted for growth based on marketing strategies implemented and walked through defects in post-implementation scenarios in different markets for business growth.

CHAPTER 16

A Business Happening Theory - Positive VS Negative

A business happening theory can be defined as a business happening that can be tracked as a defect, a business rule failure in different phases of a business cycle. A business happening can be a regular, rare or a frequent occurrence, and must be recorded and tracked immediately for a primary cause, secondary and others. The causes can be a single point or multiple point defect failures in a system. A business primary or others causes can also have dependency injections, a cause dependent on another for a ripple or a multiple effect in any area of business.

A business happening can be translated to a value using business rules positive or negative rules for a business happening. The business happening can occur a single time or multiple times and must be tracked using a business tool, to identify, a requirement failure, an implementation failure or other failures using a solution approach. A linear equation or other such equations must be created with rules for wastages using a sequential step solution approach. The business happening must be balanced as a new category type in a balance sheet using an asset or a liability category, for an appreciation or depreciation for a business happening gained or lost in an area of business. The business happenings must be documented in the business requirements digest with solution implementations. The solutions must contain balanced equations, equations showing loss or gain for a business happening.

A business happening can also be for a positive or a negative reason. The reasons for a business happening, whether positive or negative, must be monitored, and traced using an alert flag such as a messenger object where a message is triggered for a positive or a negative happening with reasons listed. A business happening must be sent to a system and an algorithm applied to retrieve solution approaches for the business happening next steps. A positive business happening can be translated to a business value earned point using a business happening translation equation and a negative traced to wastages in happening occurrences. All business happening occurrences must be documented for revisions and for use as needed.

A business happening must be ordered and ranked based on prioritization of use for business value earned and treated as a tangible or intangible asset until a category is created for a use and a purpose. The ranked values with categories must be assigned to a table or others for translation of value to a system business rule.

A negative business happening can also be translated to an economic value for a value under-utilized or for a diminished marginal value. These occurrences for happenings must be translated to an economic scale treated as util values or price values, for gain, loss or balanced values. A business happening for a scarce good with positive demand must be translated to a util value positive using a strategy to supply products to match or exceed the existing demand.

A business happening for a reason(s) listed must be computed to a current value and translated to a future value for a value earned over a period of time and if the business happening is temporary or permanent and can be discontinued based on the computation.

Part 3: Business Rule Programming Methodologies

Chapter 1

Points to Synonyms Met Methodology

Points to Synonym methodology defines the term for points earned and met for an abstraction defined. The synonyms are defined in a table containing items with points defined against each item listed in the table. These items can be features with items defined, and each item assigned points for a business abstraction defined. These synonyms can be similar or dissimilar for a business rule met, but the difference is a synonym for an approach defined using an abstraction. A map of all these synonyms met for a business rule creates a parallelism approach, a slight difference of a synonym Met for a criteria of a business rule(s) of several abstractions.

Points to Synonym Abstraction Example:

An abstraction must match several synonyms for a definition of a business construct. An abstract concept such as a business value must be translated to a definition of a business rule for a choice of several categories of abstractions for different abstract sets. The rule can be translated to several sub-rules and each rule connected to another with a synonym for a meaning of the entire abstract set. Each business rule set has points earned to add to a sum. A business rule negated must be shown as a separate abstract set negated with synonyms assigned to add to a sum. These can be abstract alternatives either earned and associated with other business rule(s).

Translated to a business programming technique:

A user story has several sub-stories with business rules that must meet the right solution approach. Each sub-story has a synonym associated with the main story for points to synonyms earned.

An array of business rules must match a primary business rule(s) for a solution. This can be defined as a business rule, 1:m, with a transition state. A state where only a partial business rule synonym is fulfilled with an uncertainty of a factor(s). A business rule is revised based on several business happenings or business occurrences.

Points to Synonym method is a programming technique that can be used using several approaches in different areas of business for points earned or accumulated for business value in different areas of business.

Chapter 2

Combinacrique Methodology

Combinacrique Methodology

An abstraction of past, present, and future time trends defined, critiqued and combined for a new abstraction for an abstract rule met. A translation of the new abstraction defined meets a trend value based on time, defines a new angle for the abstraction. The angle can be for a relation used to create a business method to earn a business value. A combine critique abstraction is defined using time trend abstractions to write comparisons and a critique review for a ***combinacrique*** methodology.

Combinacrique Abstraction Example

Combinacrique Abstraction Approach can be implemented in several ways such as for a user story approach using several combinations and approaches to validate, verify and critique a business rule defined for a business purpose.

An example is a use of a tool to compare a user story against a functional specification. A translation of the user story is a comparison of the code output or sql output against the functional specification and sql output to critique the result for the best approach used to provide a solution for a business rule used and business value earned in a user story. Another example is to compare not only the output from running the SQL query or stored procedure but to take a perspective to compare data types of internal tables against vendor tables for table synchronization.

Translated to a business programming technique:
Translation of different objects to read and receive output, a value for a best approach used for an outcome derived for a result.

CHAPTER 3

Ivy Curve Business Methodology

An ivy curve abstraction methodology is based on a difference of seasons of several ivy curves, not similar all ivies. A translation of a difference of an ivy curve is a difference of a reason, a business abstraction difference for an approach similar or dissimilar. A proof verification of the difference is the ivy curve difference rule, a rule methodology, new, to create a new differential equation using the ivy curve abstraction dimension. A map of several ivy curves similar is a method(s) used for several types of abstraction sizes, and a map single for similar maps cumulated to a sum for an entire abstraction set.

Ivy Curve Methodology Abstraction Example

An example of an ivy curve method is several products of different ivy curved defined with a similarity for a use or a need. A map of these ivies is a business value earned for a similarity or a disimilarity, for a rule fulfilled and a business value earned for use at different times of a season.

Translated to a business programming technique:

An ivy curve is an association of several product categories for a similarity such as coffee, tea, juice. These have similarities for ivies for a use and a need at different times of day and a season.

Chapter 4

Disquisition Abstraction Business Methodology

Disquisition is an abstraction technique for disquisition of a topic resulting in several topics of single or several disquisitions. A summary abstract disquisition of several topics is a content for a research construct. A note(s) collected is one way used to translate an abstract topic to create a disquisition. Several disquisitions are assembled using notes collected or literature reviewed from journals to create an abstraction. Each disquisition is a separate abstraction construct for a new disquisition abstract methodology.

Disquisition Abstraction Methodology Example:
A disquisition abstract methodology is defined using a construct for a header and content, and split into different detail points to understand the purpose and use of a disquisition.

Translated to a Business Programming Technique:
A disquisition is created for the purpose of a business function to define a business process and eliminate several manual steps. A disquisition is assembled using a summary of several steps, and a title assigned for the disquisition. The disquisition is translated to business logic based on algo-

rithms for each step of business flow. These are different disquisition methods used translate a disquisition resulting in business functions to meet a business rule(s).

CHAPTER 5

Wave Abstraction Business Methodology

A wave abstraction is defined as an abstraction using a wave approach, to identify several wave abstract concepts (waves of business rules, each an extension to create several wave abstraction rules for a combined or a complete rule). A time factor defines a wave of new and existing abstractions to compare and define a new wave abstraction.

Wave Abstraction Methodology Example:

A wave abstraction business example is use of different waves of data to test a process flow to generate a result, several. for different waves. A wave can also be used for a programming technique to create a prototype specification using waves abstraction technique.

Translated to a Business Programming Technique:

A wave abstraction programming technique is defined using data or a program in different waves (datasets, textual) to generate output (result) from a front-end or a back-end program interaction. A wave can be tested using an algorithm programmed, tested in waves (phases).

CHAPTER 6

Requirements Subtraction
Business Methodology

A requirements subtraction abstraction methodology is defined using an abstraction created with a statement and an action for a value point earned.

The requirements subtracted is based on a time factor of several variables, a difference of time value parameters, between past and present. The requirements subtraction is for a difference of time of parameters and a is value of time.

Requirements Subtraction Abstraction Methodology Example:

A requirements subtraction abstraction methodology is a methodology for an abstraction, subtracting any additional requirements not needed for an abstraction. A measure for an abstraction is used, a abstract measure translated to measuabstraq, func(x - n) for a requirement derived from a requirements subtraction method.

Translated to a Business Programming Technique:

An example of a requirement subtraction method is an abstraction of several different paragraphs revised and subtracted based on an abstraction rule.

CHAPTER 7

Practices Maximization Business Methodology

An abstract framework methodology created using business rules to standardize practices based on abstraction to maximize practices value for a use(s). The practices are maintained, tracked and revised periodically for an abstraction value of practices earned in different areas using maximization practices methodology.

Practices Maximization Abstraction Methodology Example:

A set of practices defined for a product(s) and documented in manuals. These practices are standardised and optimized based on every day practices occurrences, and translated to business happenings or occurrences, for practices revised based on practices maximization approach.

Translated to a business programming Technique:

An example is a user manual practice used by a CSR(s) in different stores. These practices are compared and revised across stores and manuals updated using practices Maximization abstraction methodology.

CHAPTER 8

Constraints Fulfillment Business Methodology

A constraint fulfillment methodology aims to fulfill a rule(s) based on several rule constraints for an abstraction defined. A constraint created and met is defined through an economic or mathematical model based on a need vs others. A constraint not fulfilled for a given abstraction results in a rule(s) not met using either a linear equation model or a mathematical model for optimization.

Constraint Fulfillment Abstraction Methodology Example:

An example of a constraint fulfillment is x number of rules which are constraints for a given business rule and a constraint y that needs to be fulfilled for the constraint fulfillment abstraction method to be true.

Translated to a Business Programming Technique:

An example is a number of business rules that need to be fulfilled with a constraint for a user story or stories and a criteria that needs to be adjusted for the business rule fulfillment to fulfill the constraint fulfillment abstraction methodology.

CHAPTER 9

Constraint Maximum Limitation Business Methodology

A constraint maximum limitation methodology determines the maximum number of constraints that can be used to limit a business rule to define an abstraction. These constraints need to be limited based on business rule criteria defined for a business rule limit. The business rule parameter constraints can be limited by data types, conversion types, for a business rule association to limit the number of data types associated with a business rule for a constraint maximization abstraction.

Constraint Maximum Limitation Abstraction Methodology Example

An example of a constraint Maximization limit for optimization is to choose the top 3-5 constraints as maximum limit for an optimal way of maximizing the constrains defined for an abstraction rule.

Translated to a business programming Technique:

An abstraction of a season I choose, I would maximize, my constraint limitation to trees, flowers, leaves for changes of seasons highlights.

A business rule must be maximized to a constraint limit of 1-3 rules for optimal business rule implementation. A business rule for number of elements for display must use a minimum number of GUI interactions of a user.

CHAPTER 10

Decision Value Business Methodology

A decision value methodology is a methodology defined for an abstraction that uses several paths to an abstraction flow for several decisions to be implemented for different business flows. The decisions for the abstraction must be derived using business rules justified with not only flows but also through prototyping, algorithm-driven, estimations based on panda algorithms, python expressions for different ways to reach a decision using different code paths. The best decision value must be selected from the options implemented for the different abstraction flows.

Decision Value Methodology Example:

A decision value earned is based on the minimum number of flows used. These include how many results are obtained based on a decision value flow.

Translated to a Business Programming Technique:

A programming technique to use different screens to route a user to different business flows vs a single flow that contains information to generate flows based on estimates.

CHAPTER 11

Pick Continuity Business Methodology

A pick continuity business methodology is a methodology defined using different types of methods for an optimal choice of a use(s) and revised periodically for continuity of use of methods for a business purpose(s). The methods are defined for different business objectives or purposes, and business methods arranged through priority ranking for a selection and use, ranked by 1...n with 1 being the top-pick method for use.

Pick Continuity Abstraction Methodology Example:

A pick continuity abstraction methodology is a choice of several options ranked and prioritized, to pick from. These options change based on requirements and business flow. A continuity is determined based on if the business flow is continued or discontinued for a business reason(s). The reasons need to be aligned next to the pick continuity abstraction table.

Translated to a Business Programming Technique:

An example is to implement defects for resolution based on the complexity of a problem to translate to different solutions chosen from a pick list of choices.

Chapter 12

Commit To Deliver Core Business Methodology

A commit to deliver Core business methodology is defined as an abstraction methodology that defines a disquisition with several rules for commitment to commit to deliver core business abstraction rules. These core abstractions are defined through commitment rules for success, failure, delay, transition state, a phase and various others.

Commit To Deliver Core Abstraction Methodology Example:
An example of a commit to deliver core abstraction methodology is a user story containing several core tasks defined with business rules for delivery. The commitment rules are defined for each core task of a user story with different definitions of commitment rules from 1..n commitments for delivery.

Translated to a business programming Technique:
An example is an abstraction of several points to earn for delivery of an abstraction based on a defined business rule. A delivery date missed for the core abstractions is cited through commitment reasons for delivery failure or success.

CHAPTER 13

Value Util Deficient
Business Methodology

A value util deficient business methodology is a methodology defined for a business rule value deficient of value utils or points earned based on the ranking and prioritization determination of a business rule determined, agreed, and justified through utils defined using a model not an estimate but a metric reported from a value util deficient.

Value Util Deficient Abstraction Methodology Example:
An example of a value-deficient util rule is a rule defined for values of use, visibility, ease, grace,,and appreciated by all.

Translated to a Business Programming Technique:
A business programming technique example is a discontinuity of use of a certain type of face powder and use of an alternative face powder based on value utils earned such as if a herb, a fruit, a color vs a chemical and various others. Utils are arranged in a matrix format from high to low.

Business Patternlet(s) Methodology - Part 4

Chapter 1

Line Pattern Business Methodology

Several leaf lines are a parallel study for a pattern similar of a topic of study(ies). These lines can also be lines in a petal, leaf or others which are variances in a study. A line indicates a path of study for a business area. Several lines, parallel, are several areas of study of a business with a difference of a business construct to complete a line(s) of a study.

A use of a line pattern is a simple linear equation for a straight line, with variances for success or failures. An example is revenue earned over a time period with variances in business occurrences. An example of a use in a business area is to generate orders for the same volume with little or no changes in price.

CHAPTER 2

Dot Patternlet Business Methodology

A dot patternlet methodology can be defined as a methodology used to connect dots to form a construct process flow for a function abstract defined for a business rule(s). The dots do not need to confirm to a particular shape type. The dots conform to a business requirement specified for a function(s). Several dots create a pattern for a requirement, a wastage, a value, a revision and others. Dots are a form of a process flow patterns and denote a definition of a process flow for a business function to match a business specification.

CHAPTER 3

Shape Pattern Methodology

A shape pattern methodology is based on different shapes of business requirements for a business rule fulfillment. A utensil made in steel, a certain shape vs a ceramic made in a standard shape. A shape pattern is used based on standard, custom, or family purpose. A shape pattern is also used for perishable products such as for cookies, pies, cakes and others. A shape is usually determined by the business owner to appeal to a customer taste(s).

CHAPTER 4

Star Pattern Methodology

A star pattern methodology is used to determine an abstraction of triangles defined in a star, a star representing a size of equal triangles. A star is used to define different abstractions to define a business rule(s) for a business fulfillment. A star topology is used create a network topology of business rules for business fulfillment. A star abstraction is defined and used for several purposes such as for a definition of several business rules, a requirement fulfillment of a product definition.

CHAPTER 5

Pattern Methodology

A patternlet methodology is defined for a business rule based on business pattern requirements such as for a best color, a whole, a partial or others. The abstraction rules are defined and determined by the business owner or the client based on tastes of a customer, a business owner to creates a rule(s) for a customer fulfillment. A business rule is dependent on a business rule fulfillment of a condition(s) to meet the pattern rules defined for a business purpose.

Chapter 6

Carrot Pattern Methodology

A carrot pattern methodology is a methodology defined for the purpose of abstraction of carrots, a size several, a pattern several, a color several. A business rule can be changed for a carrot methodology using different variable parameters. A business rule methodology is used to define an abstraction based on different types of abstraction rules for a whole.

CHAPTER 7

Leaf Pattern Business Methodology

A leaf pattern business methodology is a methodology where several different types of studies are used for a business purpose fulfillment. The business purpose can be for multiple products or services for different product channels and process flows for channels based on vendor for product type, product category, product combination, and others. These process flows are orchestrated in different leaf pattern flows which are parallel flows for customer fulfillment.

CHAPTER 8

Palm Pattern Business Methodology

A palm pattern business methodology is a set of separate studies undertaken for different types of customers. The different patterns may or may not be related, and each pattern of study uses a business flow aligned for a business requirement flow defined for a customer. A business purpose is defined for a business pattern such as temporary, permanent, a business small or medium with a focus of customers defined for a need, luxury or others. These flows exist for a purpose(s) until a new customer flow replaces the existing flow based on new customer flows.

CHAPTER 9

Rock Pattern Business Methodology

A rock pattern methodology is a product process flow where a rock is not finished, but imperfect with crevices which are dented, spotted, angled and the finish not perfect. A rock pattern is a business process flow where defects or wastages must be eliminated and processed to a finish for a business process flow and business product fulfilled with no defects for a business purpose.

CHAPTER 10

A Weave Pattern Business Methodology

A weave is synonymous with a texture, and quality for a difference of weave quality. A weave pattern in business process is a pattern where the inputs and the process defined in the weave must match a result, a weave value point earned for a weave quality. The process must be split into different categories of weaves for a weave quality texture, a weave simple, a weave several folds thick, a weave process flow split into different business process flows based on different price patterns to generate business value for the weave defined for business rule fulfillment.

CHAPTER 11

A Distortion Pattern
Business Methodology

A business methodology created with a business flow map for an input, process or output but the flow missing an algorithm not including factors for a wastage, defect, use, cost and others. A distortion occurs in some area of business, and a pattern is created until visible. These distortion patterns must be put into different business flow categories, traced and tracked in different areas of business using the distortion pattern process flow for a distortion(s) to be visible and eliminated for business flow accuracy and fulfillment.